Margaret Anne Friemel

Ben and Anna and the Birthday Present

Mit Bildern von
Barbara Hömberg

ENSSLIN

1

"Good morning, Ben," says Anna. "Happy Birthday!"
"Good morning, Anna," says Ben. "Happy Birthday!"
Ben is Anna's brother. Anna is Ben's sister.
They are twins. They are eight years old today.
"Ding, dong, ding, dong," the doorbell rings.
"It's the postman," says Anna.
"Open the door, Ben!"
"Hello, Ben," says the postman. "Here are seven birthday cards for you and Anna. Happy Birthday!"
"Thank you," says Ben and he shuts the door.
Ben and Anna are very happy.

Can you help Ben and Anna with the birthday cake?

Which is the other half of the birthday cake?

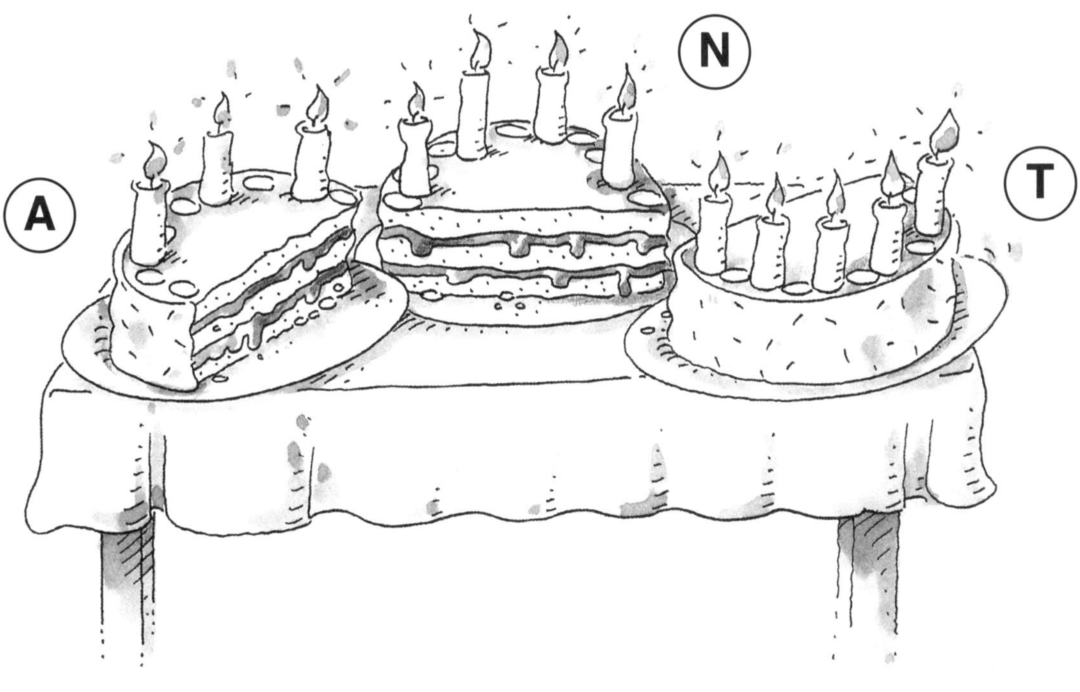

2

Look at the presents on the table:
a football for Ben and a new rucksack for Anna,
two blue pullovers from Grandma,
a game from Uncle Bob,
four books from Auntie Rita,
… but where is Uncle Fred's present?
"Wuff, wuff," says Scotty, the black and white dog.
Scotty has a small, red box in his mouth.
"Come here, Scotty," says Anna.
"Give me the box, please."
Anna opens the box.
"Look!" she says. "A toy tiger and two tickets."
She reads: "Happy Birthday to Ben and Anna!
Have fun at the circus tomorrow.
With love from Uncle Fred."

What is right?

(P) Uncle Fred gives Ben a black and white dog.

Scotty is a toy tiger. (R)

(M) Uncle Fred's present is on the table.

(H)

Uncle Fred gives Anna and Ben a circus ticket.

3

It is Saturday afternoon and Ben and Anna are at the circus.
The circus director comes into the ring.
He has a tall, black hat and a red coat.
"Hello and welcome to the circus," he says into his microphone.
"Look, Anna," says Ben. "Here come the ponies!"
Three little black ponies run into the ring.
"Hurray!" says Anna. "I love ponies."
They run and jump and then Franca, the trainer says,
"Ponies, you are very tired now!"
The ponies shut their eyes and lie down in the ring.
Franca gives each pony a big red apple.
"Clever ponies!" says Anna.

The ponies run and jump … and then?

F

E

I

4

"Please be very quiet!" says the circus director.
"Here comes Samba the tiger."
"Grrrr!" says the big tiger and jumps onto a blue box.
The trainer is not friendly.
"Samba, jump!" he says
and Samba jumps onto a brown box.
"Samba, jump!" he says again
and Samba jumps onto a yellow box.
"And now the ring of fire! Samba, jump!"
Samba does not like fire
and he does not like his trainer.
Samba opens his mouth. He has long, white teeth.
"Grrrr!" he says.
"Aaah!" says the trainer and he runs
out of the ring.
All the children clap their hands.
"Clever Samba!" they say.

Samba does not like the …

T

U X B
E
O B L

O

O W O
X Y E
L B L

L

I R G F
F E O
R N I

5

“And now Antonio and Maria and their son, Marco!” says the circus director into his microphone.
“Are they acrobats, Ben?” asks Anna.
“Yes, they are,” says Ben. “Look up, Anna!”
Anna looks up … up … up to the top of the circus tent.
She can see Antonio and Maria.
They swing and fly and jump in the air.
“They are great!” says Anna.
“Bravo!” shout the twins.
“But where is Marco?” asks Anna. “I can’t see him.”
“Look, he is with the circus director,” says Ben.
“But he isn’t happy. He is very sad.”

Can you find Marco?

6

It is nine o'clock on Monday morning.
Ben and Anna are at school.
All the children must wear school uniform:
a green pullover, a white shirt and black trousers
for the boys and a green pullover, a white blouse
and a black skirt for the girls.
Anna does not like school uniform.
The school bell rings and Miss Higgins, the teacher,
comes into the classroom with a new boy.
"Good morning, girls and boys," she says.
"Sit down, please."
"Look at the new boy, Anna," says Ben.
"It's Marco from the circus!"

Find Anna's school uniform:

A

B

T

7

After school Miss Higgins says, “Ben, come here, please. This is Marco. He is new in our class.”
“Hello, Ben,” says Marco. “I’m from the circus.”
“Hello, Marco,” says Ben. “I like the circus and the acrobats are great.”
Marco is sad. “I like the circus, too, but I don’t want to be an acrobat,” he says. “I want to train the ponies. My father is angry. He says: ‘Marco, we are all acrobats in this family!’ ”
At home Ben says, “Anna, we must help Marco.”
“I have an idea,” says Anna.
“We can speak to the circus director.”

What is right?

8

At the circus Ben and Anna see a funny clown with a red nose.
"Where is the circus director?" they ask the clown.
"Come with me," he says. "Look, there is the circus director with Alexi and his elephants."
"Please help Marco," says Anna to the circus director.
"He is very sad. He does not want to be an acrobat."
"We can ask Franca. She trains the circus ponies," says the circus director. "Come with me!"
The ponies are not tired today.
They run very fast: clip, clap, clip, clap …
"Ponies, STOP!" shouts Franca.
"Can you help Marco?" asks Ben.
"Yes, I can," says Franca.

Look at the clown!

Look at his …

shoes

M

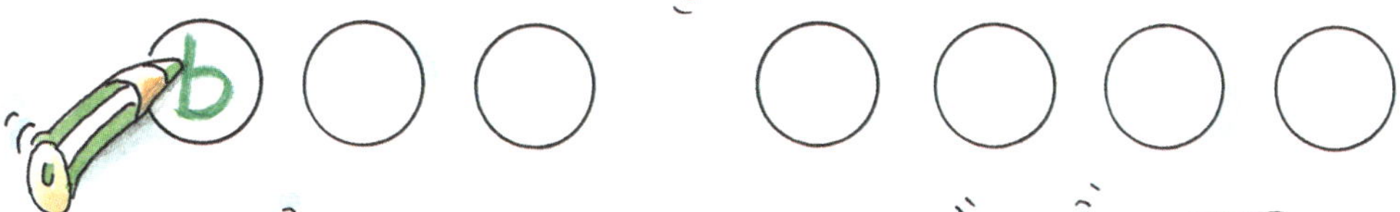

L

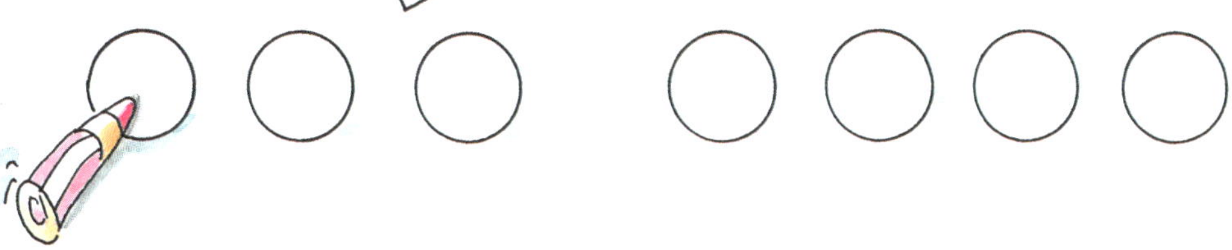

9

Franca's little black ponies are very friendly.
"Marco, you can give Nero an apple," says Franca,
"and here is a brush for you, Anna,
and a brush for you, Ben. We must clean the ponies."
The twins brush and brush and brush.
The ponies are very clean now.
"You can ride first, Anna, and then Marco and
then Ben," says Franca.
"Can we learn a circus trick?" asks Marco.
"Yes," says Franca. "That is a good idea.
You can be clowns and you can do
a circus trick with Nero."

What does Marco say?

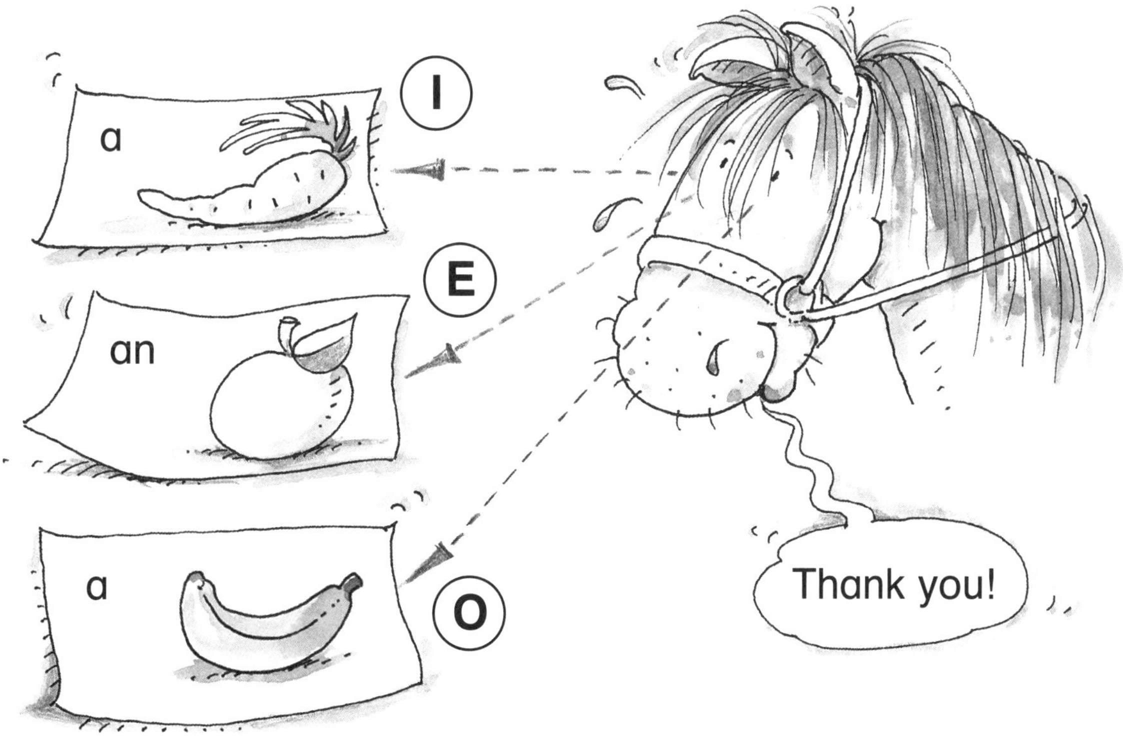

10

“Here are three clown costumes,” says Anna. “This is for you, Ben, and this is for you, Marco, and this is for me. And here are three clown masks with big red noses!”

Ben, Anna and Marco put on the costumes and the funny masks.

“We must find Franca,” says Marco. “We can do the circus trick with Nero now.”

The circus director is in the ring. He speaks into his microphone: “And now Franca and the clowns!”

“Hurray!” shout the boys and girls.

Antonio and Maria do not shout “hurray”.

“Where is Marco?” asks Antonio.

He is angry.

The masks are for …

D

C

B

11

Franca and the three clowns run into the ring.
"Hurray!" shout the girls and boys.
"And now a circus trick with Nero, the pony,"
says the circus director into his microphone.
Then Marco the clown says, "Look! Here are
three big boxes: a yellow box, a green box and
a blue box. And here is a red apple."
Marco puts the apple into the yellow box.
Then he sits on the box. Anna the clown sits on the
green box and Ben the clown sits on the blue box.
The clowns shout, "Come into the ring, Nero!
Come here and find the apple!"

What does
the clown say?

12

Nero runs into the ring. He sees Marco the clown.
He likes Marco. Marco always gives him an apple!
He runs to Marco and the yellow box.
“Please open the yellow box!” says the circus director.
Marco the clown stands up and opens the yellow box.
He takes the red apple out of the box.
“Bravo, Nero!” shout the boys and girls.
“Bravo, clowns,” shout Antonio and Maria.
“Thank you, Nero! Thank you, clowns!”
says the circus director.
“Please take off your masks now.”
Marco is very quiet. What will his mother and father say?

Where is the apple?

13

"Ooooh!" says Antonio.
"It's Marco," says Maria.
"That is a very good circus trick," says Antonio.
"I am not angry now. I am very happy.
You like the circus and you like the ponies best.
You must be a pony trainer and not an acrobat."
"Hurray!" shouts Marco.
"Hurray!" shout the twins. They take off their masks, too.
"Thank you, Anna. Thank you, Ben," says Antonio.
"You are Marco's best friends. In summer you can
come and stay with Marco at the circus."

Marco's father likes the

ponies (A)

masks (B)

circus trick (C)

14

It is the summer holidays and Anna and Ben are at the circus. Marco and his mother and father live in a big, red and white caravan.
Marco's mother puts hot spaghetti on the table for the three friends.
"Welcome to the circus, Anna and Ben," she says.
"Do you want to sleep in the caravan or in my tent?" asks Marco.
"In the tent!" shout the twins.
Near the caravan they see a small, blue tent.
"This is my tent," says Marco. "We can sleep in here."
"Hurray!" says Ben. "This is fun!"

The three friends sleep in a …

15

Marco opens the tent.
"Oh, no!" says Anna. Mick, the circus monkey, is in the tent.
"Get out of my tent!" shouts Marco.
"Eh, eh, eh!" says the monkey and he eats a banana.
The three friends go to bed at ten o'clock.
It is very quiet now.
"It is cold in the tent," says Anna. "I can't sleep."
"Girls!" say Ben and Marco and they shut their eyes and sleep.
But Anna does not sleep.
She gets up and looks out of the tent.

Anna does not sleep. Why?

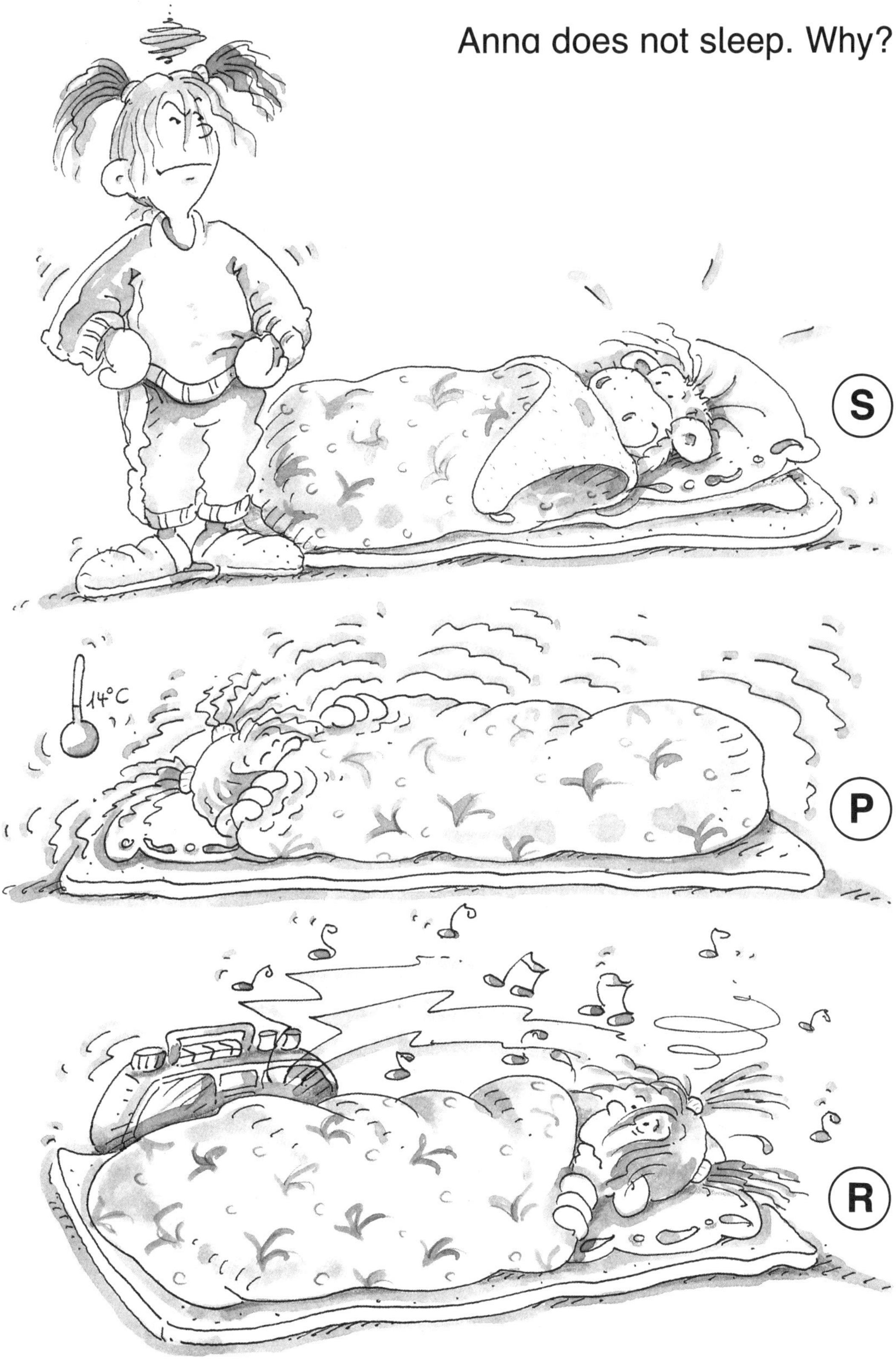

Anna can see where Franca's ponies sleep at night.
But they are not quiet tonight.
Anna can hear the ponies: they are very loud.
What's wrong with the ponies?
And what is that red light?
"Help! Help!" shouts Anna, "I can smell fire!
Ben, Marco, wake up! We must rescue the ponies."
The friends run to Franca's ponies.
They open the door and bring the ponies out.
"Look at the fire now!" says Marco.

Why does Anna shout “Help!”? Because …

(S)

… the tent
is on fire.

(B)

… the ponies
are in the tent.

(O)

… she wants
Ben and Marco
to help
the ponies.

17

“Fire! Fire!” shouts the circus director.
“Rrrr!” goes the fire alarm.
Now Franca sees the fire. “My ponies, my ponies!” she shouts. Antonio, Maria and Alexi run to the fire with buckets of water. They throw the water on the fire.
“We must have more help!” shouts the circus director.
Alexi has an idea.
“My elephants can help, too,” he says.
Alexi brings his elephants to the fire and they see the buckets full of water.
“This water is not for you – it is for the fire,” says Alexi to his elephants.

They bring water in …

18

The elephants do not drink the water.
They blow the water onto the fire.
In ten minutes the fire is out.
Toot! Toot! Toot!
Here comes a red fire engine with four firemen.
The firemen cannot see a fire.
“Where is the fire?” they ask.
“The fire is out,” says Alexi. But now
the elephants blow the water onto the firemen!
The firemen are not angry.
“Ha, ha, ha!” they laugh. Your elephants are
the best firemen here!”
they say to Alexi.

Which picture is right?

I

E

19

Franca is very happy. "Thank you, Anna and Ben. Thank you, Marco," she says.
Today is the last day of the summer holidays and it is time to say goodbye.
"Let's go to the ice-cream shop," says Franca.
"Yes, please?" asks the ice-cream lady.
"Four very big chocolate and strawberry ice-creams, please," says Franca. "And here are three red apples for the ponies!" says Marco.
"Goodbye, Anna! Goodbye, Ben!" say Franca and Marco. "See you next summer!"

Which is Anna's ice-cream?

E

D

B

S

T

You can draw

your ice-cream here:

Hast du alle Aufgaben gelöst
und die richtigen Buchstaben
in die Kästchen
nebenan eingetragen?
Dann kannst du sie
mit der Lösung vergleichen.
Aber nicht schummeln!

---

1. Auflage 2003

Ensslin-Anschrift: Harretstraße 6, 72800 Eningen
Umschlag- und Innenillustration: Barbara Hömberg
Druck: Westermann Druck, Braunschweig
ISBN 3-401-41208-6